Advent in the Home
Activities for Families

Ellen C. Becker and Mary T. Barnes
Illustrated by Phil Harber

Our Sunday Visitor Publishing Division
Our Sunday Visitor, Inc.
Huntington, Indiana 46750

Nihil Obstat: Rev. Michael Heintz
Censor Librorum

Imprimatur: ✠ John M. D'Arcy
Bishop of Fort Wayne-South Bend
June 19, 2008

The Scripture citations used in this work (with the exception of the quotation in the artwork on pages 87 and 111) are taken from the *Second Catholic Edition of the Revised Standard Version of the Bible* (RSV), copyright © 1965, 1966, and 2006 by the Division of Christian Education of the National Council of the Churches of Christ in the United States of America. Used by permission. All rights reserved.

Every reasonable effort has been made to determine copyright holders of excerpted materials and to secure permissions as needed. If any copyrighted materials have been inadvertently used in this work without proper credit being given in one form or another, please notify Our Sunday Visitor in writing so that future printings of this work may be corrected accordingly.

Our Sunday Visitor Publishing Division
Our Sunday Visitor, Inc.
200 Noll Plaza
Huntington, IN 46750

ISBN: 978-1-59276-430-3 (Inventory No. T667)
LCCN: 2008927841

Cover design: Amanda Miller
Cover photo: Shutterstock
Interior design: Lindsey Luken
Interior art: Phil Harber

PRINTED IN THE UNITED STATES OF AMERICA

DEDICATION

Newborn

Once upon a time, there was a child ready to be born.

The child asked God, "They tell me you are sending me to earth tomorrow, but how am I going to live there, being so small and helpless?"

God replied, "Among the angels, I'll choose one for you. Your angel will be waiting for you and will take care of you."

The child further inquired, "But tell me, here in heaven I don't have to do anything but sing and smile to be happy."

God said, "Your angel will sing for you and will also smile for you every day. And you will feel your angel's love and be very happy."

Again the child asked, "And how am I going to be able to understand when people talk to me if I don't know the language?"

God said, "Your angel will tell you the most beautiful and sweet words you will ever hear, and with much patience and care, your angel will teach you how to speak."

"And what am I going to do when I want to talk to you?"

God said, "Your angel will place your hands together and will teach you how to pray."

"I've heard that on the earth there are bad people. Who will protect me?"

God said, "Your angel will defend you, even if it means risking its life."

"But I will always be sad because I will not see you anymore."

God said, "Your angel will always talk to you about me and will teach you the way to come back to me, even though I will always be next to you."

At that moment, there was much peace in heaven, but voices from the earth could be heard and the child hurriedly asked, "God, if I am to leave now, please tell me my angel's name."

Her name is not important. You will simply call her "Grandma."

AUTHOR UNKNOWN

TABLE OF CONTENTS

ACKNOWLEDGMENTS

We want to thank all the parishioners of St. Jude Parish, especially the children in the parish religious-education programs and the parish school for their support of the *Advent in the Home* project.

We also wish to express our gratitude to the *Advent in the Home* committee. Their generous giving of time, talent, and energy is most greatly appreciated. They are: Ann Altena, Kim Berghoff, Julie Klingenberger, Cami Mount, Corene Rooney, and Mike and Laura Rosswurm. Our thanks also to Father Tom Shoemaker, our pastor, for his support of this project from the very beginning.

The two of us say thank you to the John Erb family, to Mary Pohlman for the time she spent proofreading the final manuscript, and to Kelley Renz, Jackie Lindsey, and George Foster for their firm commitment to this project.

Last but not least, a thank you goes out to each of our families for putting up with the late nights we put into this project. Thank you for your patience.

ELLEN C. BECKER AND MARY T. BARNES

INTRODUCTION

Advent in the Home is the result of trying to find an inviting and easy way to help families in our parish give some time, thought, and prayer to the sometimes hectic weeks preceding Christmas. Advent is the season that marks the beginning of the liturgical year and helps us focus as families on the themes of preparing the way and waiting with patient hope, joyous anticipation, and watchfulness for God-made-Man.

During the weeks leading up to Christmas, our goal was to uncover for our parishioners ways of opening their homes to the Word-made-flesh. This was the purpose of the *Advent in the Home* project at St. Jude Parish, Fort Wayne, Indiana.

More than 186 families took part in an Advent "walk through." The parish hall was transformed into a home environment by setting up a living room, kitchen and dining area, a child's play area, and a den. With soft lamp-lighting and Advent music, parishioners proceeded through each room representing the weeks of Advent. They saw first-hand various Advent wreaths, prayer reflections, and different ways to celebrate the feasts days of St. Nicholas, the Immaculate Conception, St. Juan Diego, Our Lady of Guadalupe, and St. Lucy.

Parishioners were able to see a Jesse Tree, with its symbols; an "O Antiphon House," as it would appear starting December 17, to mark the seven Messianic titles given to Christ; and a Chrismon™ Tree, with its white and gold symbolic ornaments. They saw how the family table could be set using the colors of Advent and also incorporating the parish social-action theme of "Feeding the Hungry."

These pilgrims, on their way to the manger, discovered how planting narcissus bulbs at the beginning of Advent can emphasize that before Christ came into the world, there was only darkness and sin. With His birth, Christ dispelled the darkness and brought light into the world. They experienced the Mexican tradition of luminaries, or "little fires," as a means of marking the way to the Christ Child, who is the Light of the World.

Advent in the Home presented visual examples of how parishioners could keep the Advent season holy in their own homes through prayer, games, crafts, baking, and decorating. When each family left, they were given a booklet with more than 40 different ideas or directions on how to do everything they had seen in the Advent "walk through," with the hope that it could be used as a springboard to create and develop their own Advent traditions.

Our hope is, by putting this project in book form, that we are able to help other families create Advent traditions, family treasures that are handed down from generation to generation, much like Christmas traditions. We extend our prayers and encouragement to keep the season of Advent holy by using *Advent in the Home* so that your family can be better prepared to welcome the Word into your hearts and homes at Christmas.

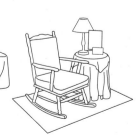

BLESSING OF THE ADVENT WREATH

This Advent wreath blessing can be used after you make your wreath but before you light the first candle. A bowl with burning incense can be put near or in the middle of your wreath. The incense is optional if you have small children, older adults, or someone who is sensitive to incense.

All present make the Sign of the Cross:

LEADER: Our trust is placed in your hands, heavenly Father.

ALL: Creator of heaven and earth.

LEADER: Father, help us prepare our hearts and homes during this Advent season for your Son.

ALL: Come, Lord Jesus!

LEADER: The winter months are here. The days are getting shorter and the nights are much longer. We need the light of your Son, Jesus, to fill us with his warmth, love, and joy. And so we gather around this wreath in preparation, anticipation, and hope in his coming as God-made-Man.

The circle shape of this wreath reminds us of the coming of Jesus, God-made-Flesh, and his unending love for us.

The light of the candles reminds us of the coming of Jesus, who is the Light of the World.

The greenery of the branches will remind us of the coming of Christ, who brings us eternal life.

Let us all who are gathered here around this Advent wreath give praise to you, O God.

Pause and then say:

You watch over us, O Lord, through darkness and light, and through each season of the heart. We praise you and thank you for your watchfulness, O Lord.

We praise you and thank you for this Advent wreath, a crown of your royal people, a symbol for us as it shines with the promise of victory over evil.

By the light of this wreath, we shall wait in patience for your Son, our Lord Jesus Christ, God-made-Man.

We are confident that he will give comfort to our sorrows and will bring hope to our wounded world.

May praise and glory always be on our lips, now and forever.

ALL: Amen.

All make the Sign of the Cross.

Sing an Advent song, such as "O Come, O Come, Emmanuel" or "I Want to Walk as a Child of the Light" by Kathleen Thomerson, or play the song "Emmanuel, God With Us" by Amy Grant.

DINNER PRAYERS FOR EACH WEEK OF ADVENT

Each night as your family gathers for dinner, light the appropriate number of candles for each week.

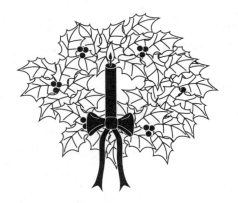

WEEK ONE (LIGHT ONE PURPLE CANDLE)

Dear Father, we ask you to hear our prayer as our family prepares for your Son's birthday. Help us to fill our hearts and home with the real meaning of Christmas. Let us always remember that Advent is a time of quiet preparation. Let us always be mindful of those in our community who will not experience quiet in their evening because of turmoil in their homes. May our hearts be open to their desire for peace. Amen.

WEEK TWO (LIGHT TWO PURPLE CANDLES)

Dear God, as we begin to decorate our home for Christmas, we thank you for this warm shelter. Let us be ever mindful of those in our community who have no home. Just as Mary and Joseph found no room at the inn, let us open our hearts in kindness and generosity to those in need of a warm and safe place to stay on these cold winter nights. Amen.

WEEK THREE (LIGHT THREE CANDLES: TWO PURPLE AND ONE PINK)

Dear Father, Jesus' birthday is fast approaching. As we prepare gifts for our family and friends, let us remember those who will find nothing under their tree. May the hopefulness of this season enter their lives. Let our hearts be generous toward their dreams and wishes. We thank you, Lord, especially for Jesus, your gift to us. Amen.

WEEK FOUR (LIGHT ALL FOUR CANDLES)

Heavenly Father, your Son Jesus' birthday is only a few days away. May his birthday bring joy and happiness to all humankind. May his peace reign throughout the world. May we be the instruments of his peace for those we meet throughout the remainder of this new liturgical year. Amen.

FROM DARKNESS INTO THE LIGHT

Plant one or more narcissus bulbs in a shallow bowl of pebbles. Fill the bowl with water until the pebbles are half covered. Place the bowl in a dark and cool place for three weeks and maintain the water level. Then move the bowl so that it has indirect light during the fourth week. When the tops of the bulbs turn green, place the bowl in direct sunlight. The bulbs should bloom just in time for Christmas. The blooming narcissus may be used as part of your Christmas table decorations!

While the family waits for signs of growth, encourage discussions about why the darkness is necessary for the development of the roots. The bulbs need this time in the darkness in order to bloom. Relate this waiting in darkness to the time when God prepared His people for the coming of His Son, Jesus Christ. With His birth, Christ dispelled the darkness and brought light into the world. Christ is the Light of the World!

THE CRÈCHE

On the First Sunday of Advent, set up your family crèche. Place only the animals and shepherds in or near the stable. Place Mary, Joseph, and the donkey in a different room at the opposite end of the house. Children can then take turns helping Mary, Joseph, and the donkey "travel" to Bethlehem by moving the figures closer to the crèche each day to a new "destination." On Christmas Eve, Mary and Joseph "arrive" in Bethlehem and are placed in the stable. On Christmas morning, gather the family around the crèche and place the star and Baby Jesus in the stable as we rejoice at His birth.

Gather around the crèche and use the following to bless your family Nativity scene.

BLESSING OF THE CRÈCHE

Read Luke 2:1-14.

LEADER: Almighty God, bless this crèche, which we display in honor of the birth of your Son, Jesus. May its presence remind our family to give you thanks and praise that Jesus has come to be one of us. Amen.

Sing "Away in a Manger" or "O Little Town of Bethlehem," or another favorite family hymn.

The same method can be used for the arrival of the Three Kings. On Christmas, place the kings in a different room and have them "travel," following the star to Bethlehem and arriving at the stable on Epiphany.

SUNDAY SCRIPTURES

Take time during the week to gather the family, perhaps around the Advent wreath, to read and discuss the upcoming Sunday Mass readings. Hearing the Word, and talking about its significance in our lives, deepens our readiness during the Advent season to receive Our Savior at Christmas.

"I baptize you with water for repentance, but he who is coming after me is mightier than I, whose sandals I am not worthy to carry; he will baptize you with the Holy Spirit and with fire."

Matthew 3:11

Even if your children are grown, your family can still study the Sunday Scriptures together. This includes seniors and singles as well. One way of doing this is by creating a blog with links to the Sunday Scriptures. Through this blog, family members can discuss the readings with one another. Creating a blog, reading the Sunday Scriptures, and sharing thoughts and insights are beautiful ways to "gather kindling" for your family Advent so that the fire of the Holy Spirit will burn brightly when you come together for your Christmas celebration.

St. Louis University has a wonderful website, www.liturgy.slu.edu, with links to the Scripture readings along with discussion questions and insights from various authors on the readings.

The readings for the Sundays of Advent may be found at www.usccb.org/nab.

FAMILY REFLECTIONS ON SCRIPTURE READINGS

FEAST OF ST. NICHOLAS
DECEMBER 6

St. Nicholas was a bishop who lived in the fourth century in a region which today is known as Turkey. As the protector of children, St. Nicholas would give gifts to young ones anonymously. By the Middle Ages, the feast day of St. Nicholas, December 6, was celebrated as a day on which children received gifts. In order to receive a gift, children would have to answer questions about their faith and recite their prayers correctly. (Those who could not would be given a piece of coal!) Today, many families celebrate the feast by having children place their shoes out the evening before. St. Nicholas fills their shoes with fruits and religious books or prayer cards.

For his feast day, find out more about the legends and stories of St. Nicholas. Pray to him for a more giving heart and temperament.

+ Make a gift from items around the house you might throw away.

+ Buy a gift or gifts for children in the hospital, a halfway house, or an abuse center, and then deliver them without fanfare.

+ Purchase new baby clothes or nursery items and donate these items to a pregnancy center or a home for unwed mothers.

ST. NICHOLAS

FEAST OF THE IMMACULATE CONCEPTION
DECEMBER 8

The feast of the Immaculate Conception celebrates Mary as the Mother of God, free from original sin from the moment of her conception. Through God's grace, Mary remained sinless throughout her life.

Honor the Blessed Virgin Mary and her role as the mother of Our Savior by celebrating the feast of the Immaculate Conception on December 8.

MARY CANDLE

Using a beautiful white candle, decorate it with symbols of Christ and place it in or on a candleholder. Cover the candle with a white

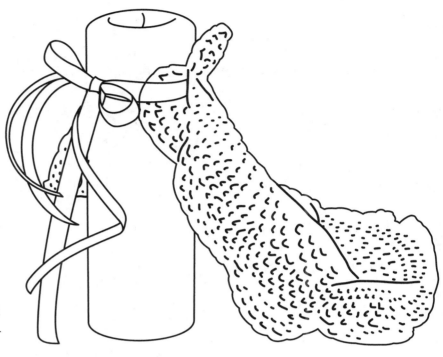

silk cloth or lace and tie this onto the candle with a ribbon. Place the candle before an image, statue, or icon of Our Lady. Gather the family around the lighted candle for prayer. Pray to Mary for her help so that we may follow her example of willingly accepting God's plan for her.

The Mary Candle illustrates the words of Isaiah: "There shall come forth a shoot from the stump of Jesse, and a branch shall grow out of his roots" (Is 11:1).

The candleholder represents Mary and also stands for the branch growing from the root of Jesse. From her womb comes the flower, the Savior of the world. The candle symbolizes Christ, who is the Light of the World. His birth scatters the world of darkness and sin. The veil, which symbolizes Mary's stainless soul, covers the candle throughout Advent. On Christmas, the veil is removed to reveal the newborn Child.

READ FROM SCRIPTURE:
Genesis 3:9-15, 20; Ephesians 1:3-6, 11-12; and Luke 1:26-38.

THE ANGELUS

LEADER: The angel of the Lord declared unto Mary;
RESPONSE: And she conceived by the Holy Spirit.

ALL: Hail Mary . . .

LEADER: Behold the handmaid of the Lord.
RESPONSE: Let it be done unto me according to your word.

ALL: Hail Mary . . .

LEADER: And the Word was made flesh,
RESPONSE: And dwelt among us.

ALL: Hail Mary . . .

LEADER: Pray for us, O holy Mother of God,
RESPONSE: That we may be made worthy of the promises of Christ.

LEADER: Let us pray.
ALL: Pour forth, we beseech you, O Lord, your grace into our hearts, that we, to whom the incarnation of Christ, your Son, was made known by the message of an angel, may by his passion and cross be brought to the glory of his resurrection, through the same Christ our Lord. Amen.

✝ Remember in a special way today your mother, grandmother, sister, aunt, neighbor, or another woman who has touched your heart in a motherly manner.

Baking for Mary's Feast Day

A special treat to celebrate the feast of the Immaculate Conception is to bake cookies that are rich in aromatic spices, such as gingerbread or molasses. Baking them on Mary's feast day, December 8, reminds us of the passage in the Book of Sirach that applies to the Blessed Virgin because of her constant and intimate association with Christ, the Incarnate Wisdom:

> *"Like cassia and camel's thorn I gave forth the aroma of spices,*
> *and like choice myrrh I spread a pleasant odor,*
> *like galbanum, onycha, and stacte,*
> *and like the fragrance of frankincense in the tabernacle."*
>
> Sirach 24:15

These cookies fill the air with rich and spicy odors, as the quoted passage speaks of Mary. This would be a wonderful activity to gather all the women in your family together and spend an afternoon in prayerful reflection on Mary's role as a woman and as a mother. Read and reflect on Scripture passages where Mary is mentioned. How does Mary's example speak to us as women and as mothers?

Read the Scripture passage from Sirach before you begin mixing the cookies, asking Mary to be with you and bless you in your work. On the next page, write down your "kitchen memories" from this year or from years past, to save — and savor — for years to come.

Molasses Cookies II
(Recipe submitted by Jan Badovinac)

- 3/4 cup shortening
- 1 teaspoon salt
- 1 cup packed brown sugar
- 2 teaspoons baking soda
- 1 egg
- 1/2 teaspoon ground cloves
- 1/2 cup light molasses
- 1 teaspoon ground cinnamon
- 2 1/2 cups all-purpose flour
- 1 teaspoon ground ginger

Directions

1. Cream together shortening and brown sugar. Stir in egg and molasses and mix well. Fold in dry ingredients and stir. Cover and chill until firm (1-2 hours).
2. Preheat oven to 350 degrees F (175 degrees C).
3. Roll dough into small balls (I use a small melon baller to help with this) and roll in white sugar. Place on lightly greased cookie sheets.
4. Bake 9-10 minutes. Leave on cookie sheet one minute until set.

OUR FAMILY'S KITCHEN MEMORIES

THE IMMACULATE CONCEPTION

CONCLUDING ROSARY PRAYER

LET US PRAY: O God, whose only begotten Son, by his life, death, and resurrection, has purchased for us the rewards of eternal life, grant, we beseech thee, that meditating upon these mysteries of the Most Holy Rosary of the Blessed Virgin Mary, we may imitate what they contain and obtain what they promise, through the same Christ our Lord. Amen.

My Rosary Book

HAIL MARY

Hail Mary, full of grace. The Lord is with thee. Blessed art thou among women, and blessed is the fruit of thy womb, Jesus. Holy Mary, Mother of God, pray for us sinners, now and at the hour of our death. Amen.

GLORY BE

Glory be to the Father, and to the Son, and to the Holy Spirit. As it was in the beginning, is now, and ever shall be, world without end. Amen.

MYSTERIES OF THE ROSARY

THE JOYFUL MYSTERIES

1. The Annunciation to Mary
2. The Visitation of Mary
3. The Nativity of Our Lord
4. The Presentation of the Lord
5. The Finding in the Temple

THE LUMINOUS MYSTERIES

1. The Baptism of the Lord
2. The Wedding Feast at Cana
3. The Preaching of the Kingdom of God
4. The Transfiguration of the Lord
5. The Institution of the Eucharist

THE SORROWFUL MYSTERIES

1. The Agony in the Garden
2. The Scourging at the Pillar
3. The Crowning With Thorns
4. The Carrying of the Cross
5. The Crucifixion of Our Lord

THE GLORIOUS MYSTERIES

1. The Resurrection of Our Lord
2. The Ascension of Our Lord
3. The Descent of the Holy Spirit
4. The Assumption of Mary
5. The Crowning of Mary as Queen of Heaven

HOW TO SAY THE ROSARY

1. Hold the crucifix and make the Sign of the Cross.
2. Say the Apostles' Creed.
3. On the first large bead, say the Our Father.
4. On the three small beads, say the Hail Mary for faith, hope, and love.
5. Think of the first mystery. Say the Our Father on the large bead. On the ten small beads, say the Hail Mary.
6. Say the Glory Be on the chain before the large bead.
7. Continue this pattern through the remaining four mysteries.
8. Finish by praying the Hail, Holy Queen, the Concluding Rosary Prayer, and then make the Sign of the Cross, blessing yourself with the crucifix.

The **Joyful Mysteries** are prayed on Mondays and Saturdays, the **Luminous Mysteries** on Thursdays, the **Sorrowful Mysteries** on Tuesdays and Fridays, and the **Glorious Mysteries** on Wednesdays and Sundays.

HAIL, HOLY QUEEN

Hail, holy Queen, Mother of Mercy, our life, our sweetness, and our hope. To thee do we cry, poor banished children of Eve; to thee do we send up our sighs, mourning, and weeping in this valley of tears. Turn then, most gracious advocate, thine eyes of mercy toward us, and after this, our exile, show unto us the blessed fruit of thy womb, Jesus. O clement, O loving, O sweet Virgin Mary.

V. Pray for us, O Holy Mother of God.

R. That we may be made worthy of the promises of Christ.

SIGN OF THE CROSS

In the name of the Father, and of the Son, and of the Holy Spirit. Amen.

APOSTLES' CREED

I believe in God, the Father almighty, creator of heaven and earth; and in Jesus Christ, his only Son, our Lord; who was conceived by the Holy Spirit, born of the Virgin Mary, suffered under Pontius Pilate, was crucified, died, and was buried. He descended to the dead; the third day he arose again from the dead. He ascended into heaven and sits at the right hand of God, the Father almighty; from thence he shall come to judge the living and the dead. I believe in the Holy Spirit, the holy catholic Church, the communion of saints, the forgiveness of sins, the resurrection of the body, and life everlasting. Amen.

OUR FATHER

Our Father, who art in heaven, hallowed be thy name. Thy kingdom come. Thy will be done on earth, as it is in heaven. Give us this day our daily bread, and forgive us our trespasses, as we forgive those who trespass against us, and lead us not into temptation, but deliver us from evil. Amen.

MY ROSARY

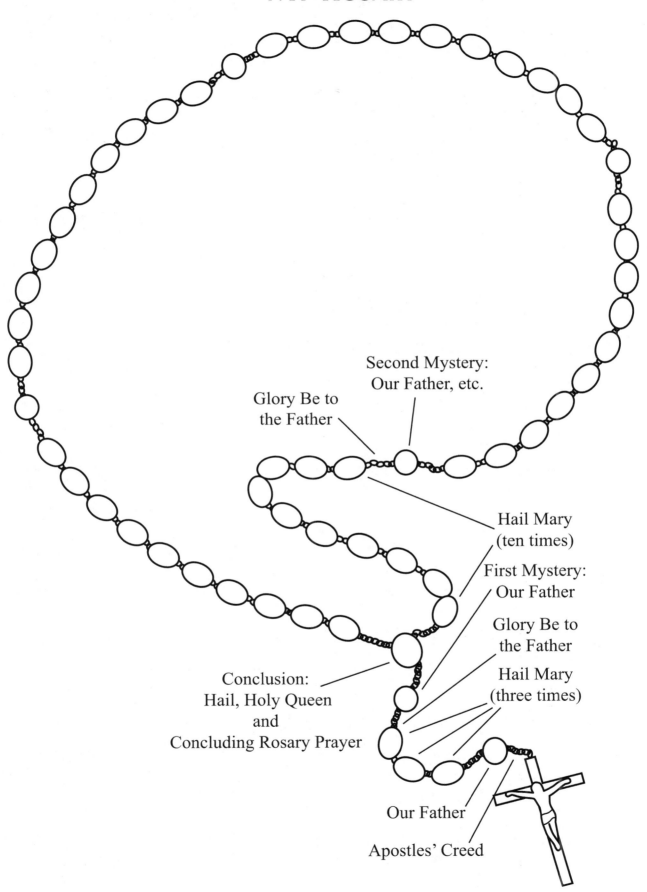

Second Mystery:
Our Father, etc.

Glory Be to
the Father

Hail Mary
(ten times)

First Mystery:
Our Father

Glory Be to
the Father

Hail Mary
(three times)

Conclusion:
Hail, Holy Queen
and
Concluding Rosary Prayer

Our Father

Apostles' Creed

"DOING GOD'S WORK" ADVENT WREATH

Advent is a time to prepare our hearts for the coming of our Savior Jesus Christ. The Advent wreath is a way for us to keep the season of Advent holy. Use the Advent wreath to help members of your family go beyond their own needs and take action on behalf of others. Each time a family member does an act of kindness for another member, color in one of the berries. When an individual member helps someone outside your family, color in a leaf. Each week, as a family, volunteer in some way to help others in your neighborhood, parish, or community. Once this social action is finished, color the appropriate candle for that week. Patterns for an Advent wreath may be found on page 27.

As a gift at Christmas, make a copy of your completed Advent wreath for every member of your family. This picture can be a reminder all year long of what it means to be God's people. A copy may also be placed in or near the crib as your family gift to the Christ Child.

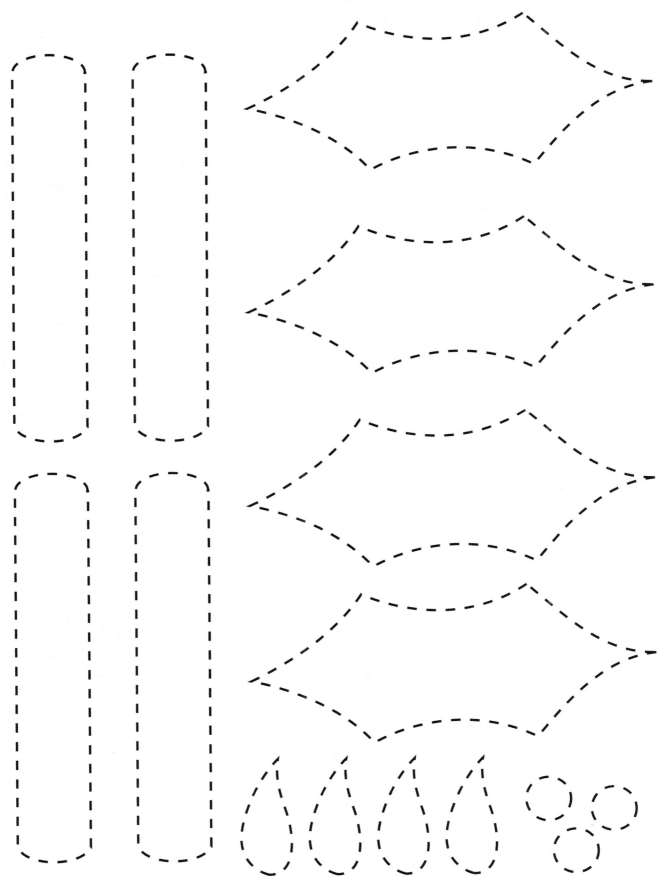

FEASTS OF ST. JUAN DIEGO AND OUR LADY OF GUADALUPE

DECEMBER 9 AND DECEMBER 12

Juan Diego, a convert to the faith, would walk 14 miles to go to Mass. On December 9, 1531, 57-year-old Juan was on his way to Mass when a beautiful lady appeared. She was dressed as an Aztec and told Juan who she was, the Immaculate Virgin Mary, the Mother of the true God. She asked Juan to help her build a shrine at Tepeyac Hill. There she would be able to show her love for the people. Mary sent Juan to the local bishop to enlist his help.

However, the bishop didn't believe Juan and asked for a sign. Mary sent Juan to the top of the hill to gather flowers. There he found roses and brought them to Mary. She wrapped the flowers in his cloak and told Juan to take the flowers to the bishop.

At the bishop's residence, Juan opened his *tilma* (cloak), and the roses fell to the floor. The bishop was surprised to see such beautiful roses in winter! Even more surprising was the image of a beautiful lady that suddenly appeared on Juan's cloak! It was the Virgin Mary! The bishop was so overtaken that he immediately fell to the floor in tears and asked the Virgin Mary for forgiveness for not believing Juan.

Mary also appeared to Juan's uncle, who was very ill, and he was cured.

For the next 17 years, Juan told the people about Our Lady of Guadalupe's message of love. He continued to live a simple and humble life, one devoted to the Eucharist, until his death. Juan Diego was declared a saint in 2002.

Above the main altar in the Basilica of Our Lady of Guadalupe in Mexico City hangs Juan Diego's cloak with the image of Our Lady.

+ Have your family act out the story of Juan Diego and Our Lady of Guadalupe.

+ Have each member of the family spread the good news of Our Lady of Guadalupe by telling someone the story of Juan Diego.

+ Display a picture of Our Lady of Guadalupe. Place roses before the image. Children may make the roses out of paper napkins or tissue paper, as shown on the next page.

PAPER ROSES

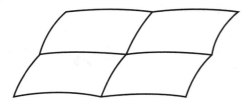

1 Unfold the napkin so that it is a single sheet or cut a piece of tissue paper 12-inches-square.

2 Taking one side of the napkin or tissue paper, fold it over about an inch and continue to roll the napkin or tissue paper into a tube.

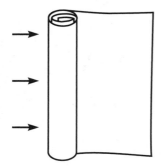

3 To size the bud, place your index finger in the top of one end of the tube to your first knuckle. Pinch the tube at this point. Then twist down the tube until fairly stiff, until about 2 inches from the bottom. This will be the stem.

4 To make a leaf, find the corner of the napkin or tissue paper at the bottom and bring it parallel with the stem. Holding the corner to the stem, unroll the rest of the tube to complete the stem, being careful not to tear the napkin or the tissue paper. At the point where the leaf ends, turn it to the inside so that the corner (leaf) wraps around the stem. Unroll the rest of the tube so that it is fairly straight.

5 Wrap the leaf around the stem, pinch, and continue to twist. Find the tip in the middle of the bud and twist to form the rose.

OUR LADY OF GUADALUPE

"ADVENT BLESSINGS BOOK"

Our Heavenly Father has shown His unending love for us by sending His only Son to walk among us and to eventually die to save each of us. We must never forget the connection between the wood of the crib and the wood of the cross. There has been no greater blessing bestowed upon us from God. We need to always give thanks and praise to Him for the gift of His Son to the world. One way to do this is to count how God continues to shower us with blessings each day during the season of Advent.

We can do this by keeping an "Advent Blessings Book." When it is convenient for your family to gather around the crèche, write down in the "Advent Blessings Book" three ways your family has been blessed over the preceding 24 hours. When these three blessings have been noted, pass the book to each person. Space has been allocated for each person to write down three personal blessings. Everyone will see in very concrete terms how each member of the family has been blessed in at least six different ways in only one day.

If your family would do both, family blessings and individual blessings for each day during Advent — with 22 days being the shortest and 28 days being the longest Advent season — each person in your family would be blessed by God anywhere from 132 times to 168 times by Christmas Day.

On the day before Christmas, review the list of blessings bestowed on your family during the Advent season. This is a wonderful way to prepare for Mass, the hallmark of giving thanks and praise to God.

This spiritual exercise can be used for all the weeks of the liturgical year. It also points out one of the important purposes of our Sunday obligation: we have an obligation to give thanks and praise for the many ways God blesses us each week.

Family members can see very clearly why each person has an obligation to be present with the community, not only on Christmas Day but each Sunday of the year, to give thanks and praise to God for blessing themselves and their families in so many different ways. This exercise can give us a better perspective on why we come to church and join our prayer of thanksgiving with the entire Church family.

When each book is completed, it may be placed near the crèche or hung on the tree, or copies may be given to each family member as an Advent memory.

(Originally published in *Catechist* magazine, January 2008, as "Don't Forget to Count Your Blessings," by Mary T. Barnes.)

Saturday — Family Blessings

_____

_____

_____

Saturday — Individual Blessings

_____

_____

_____

_____

Advent Blessings Book

First Week

Thursday — Family Blessings

_____

_____

_____

Thursday — Individual Blessings

_____

_____

_____

Monday — Family Blessings

_____

_____

_____

Monday — Individual Blessings

_____

_____

_____

Sunday — Family Blessings

_____
_____
_____
_____

Sunday — Individual Blessings

_____
_____
_____
_____

Friday — Family Blessings

_____
_____
_____
_____

Friday — Individual Blessings

_____
_____
_____
_____

Tuesday — Family Blessings

_____
_____
_____
_____

Tuesday — Individual Blessings

_____
_____
_____
_____

Wednesday — Family Blessings

_____
_____
_____
_____

Wednesday — Individual Blessings

_____
_____
_____
_____

Saturday — Family Blessings

_____

_____

_____

Saturday — Individual Blessings

_____

_____

_____

Advent Blessings Book

Second Week

Thursday — Family Blessings

_____

_____

_____

Thursday — Individual Blessings

_____

_____

_____

Monday — Family Blessings

_____

_____

_____

Monday — Individual Blessings

_____

_____

_____

Sunday — Family Blessings

_____

_____

_____

_____

Sunday — Individual Blessings

_____

_____

_____

_____

Tuesday — Family Blessings

_____

_____

_____

Tuesday — Individual Blessings

_____

_____

_____

_____

Friday — Family Blessings

_____

_____

_____

_____

Friday — Individual Blessings

_____

_____

_____

_____

Wednesday — Family Blessings

_____

_____

_____

Wednesday — Individual Blessings

_____

_____

_____

_____

Saturday — Family Blessings

_____

_____

_____

Saturday — Individual Blessings

_____

_____

_____

Advent Blessings Book

Third Week

Thursday — Family Blessings

_____

_____

_____

Thursday — Individual Blessings

_____

_____

_____

Monday — Family Blessings

_____

_____

_____

Monday — Individual Blessings

_____

_____

_____

Sunday — Family Blessings

_____

_____

_____

_____

Sunday — Individual Blessings

_____

_____

_____

_____

Friday — Family Blessings

_____

_____

_____

_____

Friday — Individual Blessings

_____

_____

_____

_____

Tuesday — Family Blessings

_____

_____

_____

Tuesday — Individual Blessings

_____

_____

_____

Wednesday — Family Blessings

_____

_____

_____

Wednesday — Individual Blessings

_____

_____

_____

Saturday — Family Blessings

_____

_____

_____

Saturday — Individual Blessings

_____

_____

_____

Advent Blessings Book

Fourth Week

Thursday — Family Blessings

_____

_____

_____

Thursday — Individual Blessings

_____

_____

_____

Monday — Family Blessings

_____

_____

_____

Monday — Individual Blessings

_____

_____

_____

Sunday — Family Blessings

_____

_____

_____

_____

Sunday — Individual Blessings

_____

_____

_____

_____

Friday — Family Blessings

_____

_____

_____

_____

Friday — Individual Blessings

_____

_____

_____

_____

Tuesday — Family Blessings

_____

_____

_____

_____

Tuesday — Individual Blessings

_____

_____

_____

_____

Wednesday — Family Blessings

_____

_____

_____

_____

Wednesday — Individual Blessings

_____

_____

_____

_____

FEAST OF ST. LUCY
December 13

Lucy (Lucia) was a young girl who lived in Sicily about A.D. 300. Lucy was persecuted and tortured, eventually being blinded and killed, because she would not give up her Christian beliefs. The lengthening of days and the return of light were celebrated by winter festivals held annually by *Scandinavian* people in honor of St. Lucy. The legends surrounding St. Lucy were brought to Scandinavia by Italian sailors.

Custom held that the eldest daughter in the family was dressed as St. Lucy in a white gown, red sash, and a crown of green leaves and candles. Coffee and cake greeted the members of her family as she awakened them from their sleep. Carrying candles and small cakes, which were called "Lucia's Buns," "Lucia's sisters" would join her, and together they would travel from home to home in their neighborhood. To each home they brought a little of the warmth and light that was soon to come into the world. Lucia's light was seen as a reflection of the greater Light of the World, Jesus Christ.

Use the feast of St. Lucy to decorate your home with lights. Lights used in windows or on mantles, luminaries along your walkway, Christmas Tree lights, or even your porch light can be kept dark from the beginning of Advent and then turned on December 13 to celebrate her feast day.

CHRISTMAS LIGHTS
Use the feast of St. Lucy to bring the warm and gentle light of the Advent season into your home. Read a story of St. Lucy and pray to her before you place your lights on your Christmas Tree and in your windows.

An *Irish* tradition is to place a tall candle in the window to light the path for the Holy Family. It is customary for the youngest child in the family to light the candle because, as the Irish point out, he or she will live the longest and pass along the custom the furthest.

CHRISTMAS WHEAT
A *Hungarian* custom on the feast of St. Lucy is to plant Christmas wheat. Pressed gently into a pot of garden soil, watered, and kept in a moderately warm room, the wheat will be sprouted soft green by Christmas. Then the children in the family may carry the wheat to the crèche as a gift for the Baby Jesus.

✚ Plan a visit to a neighbor or relative on or near December 13. Bring along cookies or a special treat, or make St. Lucia's Crown to share (page 44).

ST. LUCIA'S CROWN

- One 1 lb. loaf of frozen bread dough
- yellow food coloring
- sliced almonds
- green and red candied cherries
- 1 cup confectioners' sugar
- 1 tbsp. water

DIRECTIONS

1. Thaw the bread according to directions. Work with the dough at room temperature on a clean, unfloured surface. Divide the loaf into 4 equal sections. Gently knead in 1 drop of yellow food coloring on each section. Roll each of **3** sections into a 22-inch strand. Braid the strands and place on a greased baking sheet (a round stone works well for this). Form the braid into a circle and pinch the ends to seal.

2. Gently knead 1 drop of yellow food coloring into the remaining dough. Divide the dough into 3 equal sections. Roll each section into a 12-inch strand. Braid the strands and place on a separate greased baking sheet. Form the braid into a circle, pinching the ends to seal.

3. Cover. Place in a warm, draft-free location. Let rise until double.

4. Bake at 350 degrees for 25-30 minutes. Cool on a wire rack. When cool, make 6 holes in the small braid for the candles. Drizzle each braid with icing. Place the small braid in the center, on top of the large braid. Decorate with sliced almonds and candied cherries. Insert the candles in the top braid.

5. To make the icing: Mix the confectioners' sugar with 1 tbsp. water. Icing may be thinned by adding water for the desired consistency.

OPTION

If preferred, any recipe for white bread may be used. Before adding the additional flour, mix in 1/4 cup citron, 1/4 cup chopped, blanched almonds, and 1/2 tbsp. lemon peel. Then knead, let rise, and divide as explained above.

ST. LUCY

YOUR FAMILY CHRISTMAS TREE

The month of December can be a hectic time for families preparing for the Christmas season. One way to slow the pace, and to experience the season of Advent as a time of anticipation and longing, is to decorate your Christmas Tree in stages.

Put your Christmas Tree up the first part of December, but let it remain bare of any decorations for a week. On the feast of St. Lucy, December 13, read a brief story of St. Lucy and pray the following prayer to her:

Dear St. Lucy, as our family puts the Christmas lights on this evergreen, let us be mindful of how we must shine the light of Christ throughout the world. May your life be an example of the courage we must have to carry out this mission of spreading the Good News to the rest of the world. Amen.

Then decorate your tree with lights, and place lights in your windows and anywhere in your home that is usually decorated with lights. Wait a few more days or another week before placing your ornaments on the tree. Blessing the ornaments before they are placed on the tree reminds us of each one's unique and special story. Have each member of the family choose a special ornament and hold it while another member blesses the ornaments.

BLESSING OF THE ORNAMENTS

LEADER: God, we ask you to bless these ornaments. Each one of these ornaments represents a thread in the tapestry of our family's life together. We gather today to be mindful of how you have been present with us through all our days. We know that you are present with us now as our family story continues to unfold. Help us to see one another as precious and dear, to treat one another with tenderness and care, and to enjoy and celebrate the joy that each one of us brings to our family. We ask this in a spirit of memory and celebration.

ALL: Amen.

After the blessing, as you hang each ornament, share the story or memory connected to that ornament. Have a special food/drink that is reserved for hanging the ornaments on the tree.

AN ADVENT CALENDAR

The Advent calendar is a German invention that was originally designed to involve children in the celebration of the days leading up to Christmas. The calendar usually has small flaps, one of which is opened on each day of Advent. Behind each flap is an image or motif signifying the season.

Today, many types of Advent calendars are available. You may make your own or purchase one at most Christian bookstores. Children can use the calendars to help them visually count down the days until the birth of Our Lord, while keeping the focus on the holiness of the season.

Many of the commercial Advent calendars have a total of 24 flaps. Keep in mind, though, that the liturgical season of Advent does not always follow the calendar month of December and may have more or less days than 24. To truly celebrate Advent as a holy season, count the actual number of days in Advent and use that as the marker for counting down the days before Christ's birth.

Use the Advent calendar in conjunction with the Jesse Tree in establishing a family Advent tradition. Read the Scriptures for the Jesse Tree (pages 57-58), one each day as part of the Advent calendar.

ADVENT IN THE PARISH

Within your parish community there are opportunities to celebrate the season of Advent. Be aware of the opportunities for spiritual growth and service to the community provided by your parish or diocese by reading the bulletin and reviewing the links on the parish or diocesan website. As a family, and as individuals, plan in advance some ways to prepare for the beautiful season of Advent.

THE GIVING TREE

Many parishes set up a "Giving Tree" during Advent, to help those who might be in need of assistance. Tags with ideas for gifts are placed on the tree, along with requests for monetary gifts to aid in paying utilities, groceries, and so on. Parishioners take a tag from the tree, buy the gift requested, and bring the gift back to church on the appointed weekend. If your parish doesn't already have a Giving Tree, perhaps you can suggest putting one up.

Another way of doing this in your own home is to have a small tree and each day place a tag with a good deed that has been completed, as a gift to the Christ Child for Christmas.

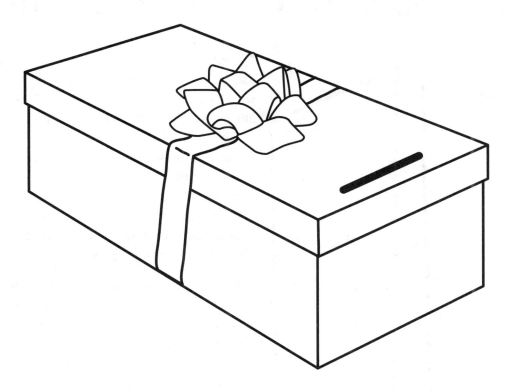

A GIFT FOR BABY JESUS

Children can get caught up in the hustle and bustle of the days leading up to Christmas just as much as adults. One way to help children keep the season of Advent holy is to have them prepare a gift for the Christ Child.

Take a shoe box and wrap it with whatever paper and ribbon the children think is the most beautiful. After the box is wrapped, cut a slit in the top that is large enough to allow a coin wrapped in a note to fall through the hole and into the box. Take the box and put it near your family crèche.

Each evening at the dinner table, as part of your Advent Dinner Prayer, have each person — Mom and Dad included — share one good deed that has been done for Jesus that day. Have Mom or Dad or an older sibling write the good deed on a small piece of paper. Take a penny, nickel, or dime, depending on the age of the participants, and wrap the "good deed" paper around the coin. While singing "O Come, O Come, Emmanuel," have each member of the family take his or her "gift" and put it in the box for Baby Jesus.

When your family attends church on Christmas Day, take the gift prepared for the Christ Child and have the youngest member of your family place it by the crib in your parish.

THE SACRAMENT OF RECONCILIATION

The most beautiful gift we can give to Christ is a humble and contrite heart. A wonderful way to prepare for Christ's coming during Advent is to meet Him in the Sacrament of Reconciliation. Many parishes offer a parish reconciliation service during this liturgical season. A communal penance service provides a great opportunity for families to gather in prayer. Watch your parish bulletin for times in your home parish for the communal service or times for individual confessions.

Individuals and families can prepare for the Sacrament of Reconciliation during Advent by using Scripture verses in a simple prayer service, focusing on the themes of the season. This can be done the week prior to receiving the Sacrament of Reconciliation.

RECONCILIATION PRAYER SERVICE

At the end of the day, gather around the crèche for this short prayer service.

An adult lights a candle.

All present make the Sign of the Cross.

LEADER: Give thanks to God for he is good.

ALL: He gave us Jesus, his only Son, to be with us. His love endures forever.

READER: A reading from . . . *(Here the Scripture passage for the day is read.)*

This is followed by sharing insights based on the discussion and examination-of-conscience questions that follow the Scripture passages on the next page.

QUESTIONS FOR DISCUSSION AND EXAMINATION OF CONSCIENCE

First Evening: John 8:12

- How can we keep Jesus' light burning brightly inside ourselves?

- What have I done today to keep Jesus' light burning brightly inside me?

- Do I ever act like Jesus is not my light?

Second Evening: Isaiah 9:2

- What does it mean to "walk in darkness"?

- How have I shown others I thought of Jesus today?

- How have I acted in a dark way today, as if I didn't know or care about Jesus?

Third Evening: Luke 1:5-25

- What does it mean and why is it important to keep a promise?

- How have I kept my promises to others today?

- How have I been unfaithful to my word given to others?

Fourth Evening: Luke 1:26-35

- What do the words "Do not be afraid" and "The Lord is with you" mean?

- Have I trusted in the Lord today, as Mary did?

- Have I shown a lack of courage in being a Catholic today?

Fifth Evening: Luke 2:8-20

- Why do you think God chose the shepherds to be the first persons to hear news about the birth of God's Son?

- How have I been open to the poor and to people on the fringe of society?

- How have I failed to stand up against injustice today?

Sixth Evening: Luke 2:6-7

- What does it mean that the season of Advent is a time to prepare our hearts for Jesus?

- How have I shown warmth and comfort to others so that Jesus can truly find a place in my heart to lay His head?

- How have I failed to give a smile or use gentle words with others?

Seventh Evening: Matthew 2:1-12

- What does it mean to stretch and search your mind, heart, and soul?

- How have I been like the Wise Men in keeping a lookout for the ways God has worked in my life today?

- How have I failed to be an instrument of God's love for others today?

"GOD SO LOVED THE WORLD"
PAPER CHAIN

Every child enjoys creating a paper chain. This activity involves cutting out the 28 Advent Bible verses below and gluing each verse to a separate paper link. A new Advent Bible verse is to be read each day of Advent and then added to the paper chain.

DIRECTIONS

Cut out a verse. Find the verse in the Bible and read it. Glue that verse to a paper chain link. Use purple paper for the first, second, and fourth weeks, and pink paper for the third week. The paper chain grows during the season of Advent, just as our hearts and homes should "grow open" for the coming of Baby Jesus. Use the paper chain as a decoration in a child's room or on the family Christmas Tree. You can also use these verses for an Advent calendar. Read and glue one verse each day to a calendar, counting down the days until the birth of Christ.

JOHN 1:1	MATTHEW 1:20-21	LUKE 2:11-12
ISAIAH 7:14	LUKE 1:32-33	LUKE 2:16-17
LUKE 1:5-7	MATTHEW 24:42	MATTHEW 2:1-2
LUKE 1:8-13	MICAH 5:2	MATTHEW 2:9-11
LUKE 1:14-20	LUKE 2:4-5	JOHN 1:14
DANIEL 7:13-14	LUKE 2:6-7	JOHN: 13:34
LUKE 1:26-28	JOHN 1:1-2	JOHN 18:37
LUKE 1:30-31	JOHN 1:9	LUKE 2:14
LUKE 1:41-42	ISAIAH 9:6	
MATTHEW 1:22-23	LUKE 2:8-10	

Pattern for Paper Chain Links

CHRIST WITHIN US

Use the four weeks of Advent to examine how Christ lives in us and through us. Using the questions below will help us prepare for His coming, so that Christ may dwell in our hearts, with His light shining forth from us.

Write the questions on index cards and label with the appropriate week. Put the cards in a conspicuous place where all family members will be able to read the cards daily. The refrigerator or bulletin board would be an ideal location.

Each family member should spend 10 to 15 minutes a day reflecting on the questions for the week. If so desired, the reflections may be written in a journal. This is a good way to remember your insights and expand on your thoughts. As a family, designate a special time (perhaps before or after the meal, whenever the weekly Advent prayer is used — see page 9) to discuss the questions and reflections.

QUESTIONS AND REFLECTIONS

WEEK 1: MY RELATIONSHIP WITH MYSELF
- How do I perceive myself?
- What short-term and long-term goals have I set for myself?
- Do I attempt to do my best in all things?
- Am I becoming the person God created me to be?

WEEK 2: MY RELATIONSHIP WITH MY FAMILY AND FRIENDS
- How well do I get along with my family and friends?
- Am I a good and true friend?
- Do I help and encourage my family members and friends?

WEEK 3: MY RELATIONSHIP WITH MY CHURCH
- Do I give generously of my time, talent, and treasure?
- Do I serve others?
- Where does my faith fit in my life?

WEEK 4: MY RELATIONSHIP WITH GOD
- Do I pray on a daily basis?
- How do I perceive God?
- Are others able to see His love in my actions, attitudes, and behavior?
- Am I proud to profess my faith?

This is another activity that would lend itself to a family blog if members are separated by geographical distance.

THE JESSE TREE

The Jesse Tree is named from Isaiah 11:1:

There shall come forth a shoot from the stump of Jesse, and a branch shall grow out of his roots.

The "Jesse Tree" is the story of our salvation, and the symbols depict the "Messianic" line, from Genesis to the birth of Christ. It is a tradition that dates back to the Middle Ages. The ornaments are colorful and are placed on the tree daily, throughout Advent, after reading the corresponding Scripture passage. The Jesse Tree can stand alone as a religious exercise for private use or as an act of prayer in a communal setting. The Jesse Tree may be used in conjunction with another family ritual, such as the lighting of the Advent wreath. As your family reads the Scripture stories, God's plan of redemption will unfold, and the awareness of God's saving love for us through the gift of His only Son, Jesus Christ, our Savior, will become more profound. We can be inspired by the stories we read, and thereby enrich our own faith.

A Jesse Tree can be made in a number of ways: by hanging ornaments on a bare tree branch set into a stand or pot; by velcroing fabric, felt, or embroidered ornaments onto a banner; or by hanging the ornaments on a traditional Christmas Tree.

There are many ways to celebrate this Advent tradition. We have given but a few suggestions for you to start this simple prayer experience with your family. Be creative in how you make your ornaments and in choosing the Scripture passages most appropriate for you and your family.

BREAD DOUGH RECIPE
Use this recipe to make your Jesse Tree or Chrismon™ Tree ornaments.

- 2 cups baking soda
- 1 cup flour
- 1 1/4 cup water

DIRECTIONS
1. Mix the 3 ingredients in a saucepan.
2. Heat over medium heat, stirring often until the mixture has the consistency of moist mashed potatoes.
3. Put the dough on a plate and allow it to cool.
4. Cover the dough with a damp cloth and allow it to cool to handling temperature.
5. Turn the dough onto the counter and knead it until it's smooth.
6. Roll the dough out to approximately 1/4 inch thick and cut as desired.
7. Bake at 325 degrees F. Cool in the oven (*this is important*).
8. Decorate the pieces as desired, finishing with a coat of varnish, acrylic, nail polish, or white glue mixed with a little water. The point is to waterproof the ornaments so that moisture doesn't make them soft and tacky.

JESSE TREE SCRIPTURE VERSES
(THE SYMBOLS AND READINGS ARE ONLY SUGGESTIONS.)

FIRST WEEK OF ADVENT

SUNDAY
Isaiah: *Isaiah 9:6*
Symbols: branch, tree

MONDAY
Creation: *Genesis 1:1—2:3*
Symbols: dove, earth, sun, moon, stars

TUESDAY
Adam and Eve: *Genesis 3:8-24*
Symbols: Tree with fruit, apple, man, woman

WEDNESDAY
Noah: *Genesis 6:14-22*
Symbols: ark, animals, dove, rainbow

THURSDAY
Abraham: *Genesis 15:1-6*
Symbols: torch, sword, mountain

FRIDAY
Isaac: *Genesis: 17:15-19; 21:1-6*
Symbols: bundle of wood, altar, ram, smiling face

SATURDAY
Jacob: *Genesis 28:10-22*
Symbols: ladder, kettle

SECOND WEEK OF ADVENT

SUNDAY
Joseph: *Genesis 45:4-20*
Symbols: sack of grain, well, silver coins, coin bag, tunic

MONDAY
Moses: *Exodus 3:1-5*
Symbols: baby in basket, river/rushes, burning bush, stone tablets

TUESDAY
Israelites: *Exodus 12:1-14*
Symbol: lamb

WEDNESDAY
Joshua: *Joshua 6:2-5*
Symbols: ram's horn, trumpet

THURSDAY
Gideon: *Judges 7:19-20*
Symbol: clay water pitcher

FRIDAY
Ruth: *Ruth 1:7-8; 15-18; 2:17-19*
Symbol: sheaves of wheat

SATURDAY
Samuel: *1 Samuel 3:7-10*
Symbols: crown, lamp, temple

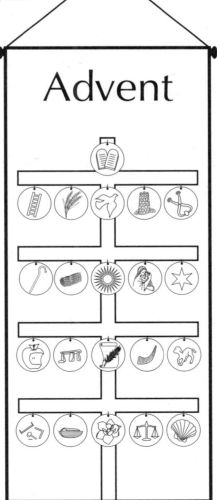

Advent

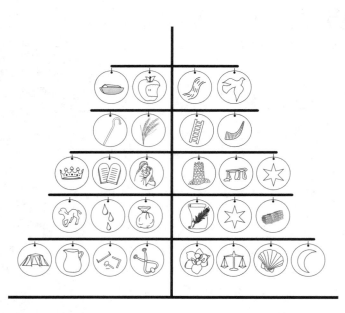

SUNDAY
Nehemiah: *Nehemiah 6:15-16*
Symbol: city wall

MONDAY
John the Baptist: *Matthew 3:4-6*
Symbol: scallop shell

TUESDAY
Elizabeth: *Luke 1:39-56*
Symbol: mother and child

WEDNESDAY
Zechariah: *Luke 1:57-80*
Symbol: pencil and tablet

THURSDAY
Joseph: *Matthew 1:18-25*
Symbols: hammer, carpenter's square, saw

FRIDAY
Mary: *Luke 1:26-38*
Symbols: white lily, rose, crown of stars, pierced heart

SATURDAY
Jesus: *Luke 2:1-20*
Symbols: star, manger, Chi-Rho

THIRD WEEK OF ADVENT

SUNDAY
David: *1 Samuel 16:11-13*
Symbols: shepherd's crook, harp, slingshot, six-pointed star

MONDAY
Solomon: *1 Kings 3:5-14; 16-28*
Symbols: scales of justice, temple

TUESDAY
Elijah: *1 Kings 18:17-39*
Symbol: stone altar

WEDNESDAY
Hezekiah: *2 Chronicles 29:15-19*
Symbol: tent

THURSDAY
Isaiah: *Isaiah 6:1-13*
Symbol: tongs with hot coal

FRIDAY
Jeremiah: *Jeremiah 1:4-10*
Symbol: tears

SATURDAY
Habakkuk: *Habakkuk 1:1—2:1*
Symbol: stone watchtower

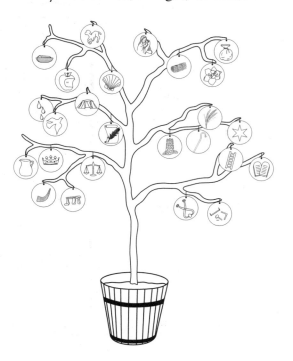

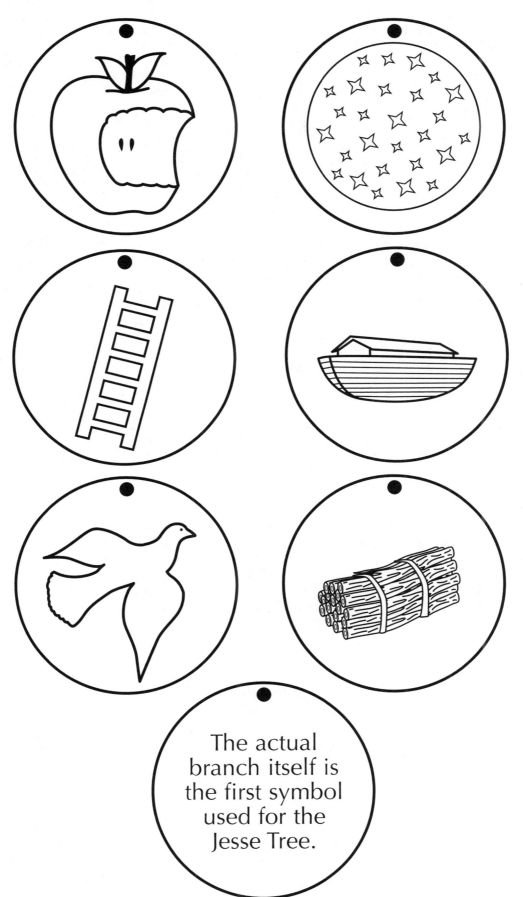

The actual branch itself is the first symbol used for the Jesse Tree.

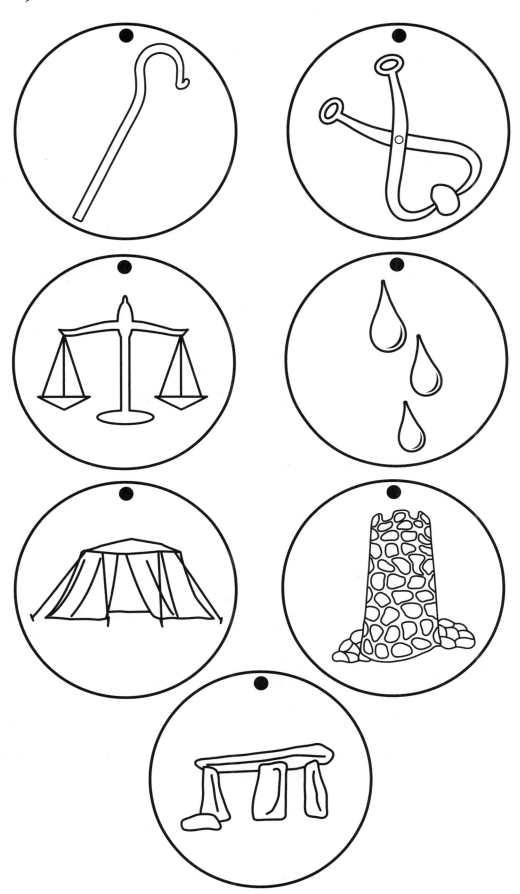

JESSE TREE

O ANTIPHON HOUSE

THE O ANTIPHONS

December 17 marks the beginning of the "O Antiphons," the seven jewels of our Advent liturgy, dating back to the fourth century, one for each day until Christmas Eve. These antiphons — each beginning with the interjection "O" — address Christ with seven Messianic titles, based on the Old Testament prophecies and types of Christ.

The O Antiphons are the verses for the ancient hymn "O Come, O Come, Emmanuel." The first letter of the Messianic titles — *Emmanuel, Rex, Oriens, Clavis, Radix, Adonai, Sapientia* — spell out the Latin words *ERO CRAS* ("Tomorrow, I will come"). The antiphons are part of the Evening Prayer of the Liturgy of the Hours (Divine Office). They are also used as the alleluia verse before the Gospel at Mass during these seven days of Advent.

DIRECTIONS

An "O Antiphon House" can be created by cutting a house out of flat cardstock. Another version would be to create a tower out of cardstock.

The house/tower will have eight hinged windows. Under each window will be the appropriate symbol for the O Antiphon symbol of the day. A ninth window located at the top of the house/tower will reveal the Nativity scene to be opened on Christmas Day. The windows are opened one by one each day at the singing of the antiphon, or incorporated during the Christmas Novena.

1. Use two sheets of colored poster board. Draw a design of the house/tower on the poster board. Cut out the design.
2. Use the top piece of board to draw eight small square windows and one large window for Christmas Day. The size of all the windows should be the same, about 1 inch to 1 1/4 inches square. The one large window, for Christmas Day, should be larger, about 2 inches square. This window is the largest and will be opened last. It should be centered at the top of the house/tower. Use the O Antiphon symbols as a guide to determine the size of the windows. Decorate the outside of the house/tower.
3. Number the eight windows from 17 to 24. The ninth, larger window at the top of the house/tower is numbered 25. The O Antiphon symbols can be colored by the children to show through the windows. Use a Nativity scene from an old Christmas card for the large window, which is to be opened on Christmas Day. Suggested scenes: Madonna and Child, Jesus in the manger, or the Holy Family in the stable — or have the children draw and color their own Nativity scene.
4. Each picture should be about 1/4 inch larger than the window so that no edges can be seen in the window. Place the top sheet on a cutting board. Carefully cut the top, bottom, and middle of each window, but not the sides, so that each window has "shutters" to open. Or a simpler way is to cut three sides to each window, but not the fourth side, leaving it intact to act as a hinge. With the bottom sheet under the top, using a pencil, lightly mark the outline of the squares through the windows. Cut out the pictures of the O Antiphons and glue them to the bottom poster board over the appropriate squares.
5. Carefully glue the two pieces of poster board together around the edges. Use large paper clips or clothespins to hold the layers together until the glue is completely dry.
6. Display the O Antiphon House (or Tower) wherever the family will gather for prayer.
7. Starting on December 17, open the pertinent window each day, read the Bible passage that goes with the antiphon, and sing the corresponding verse from "O Come, O Come, Emmanuel."

SCRIPTURE VERSES FOR THE O ANTIPHON HOUSE

DECEMBER 17: *O SAPIENTIA*
Jesus is *Wisdom*: Wisdom 8:1
Symbols: oil lamp, open book, dove

DECEMBER 18: *O ADONAI*
Jesus is *Lord and Ruler*: Exodus 3:2; 20:1-17
Symbols: burning bush, stone tablets

DECEMBER 19: *O RADIX JESSE*
Jesus is the *Root of Jesse*: Isaiah 11:1-3
Symbols: flower, plant with flower

DECEMBER 20: *O CLAVIS DAVIDICA*
Jesus is the *Key of David*: Isaiah 22:22
Symbols: key, broken chains

DECEMBER 21: *O ORIENS*
Jesus is the *Rising Dawn*: Psalm 19:4b-6
Symbols: sunrise, sun

DECEMBER 22: *O REX GENTIUM*
Jesus is the *King of the Nations*: Psalm 2:7-8
Symbols: crown, scepter

DECEMBER 23: *O EMMANUEL*
Jesus is *Emmanuel*: Isaiah 7:14; 33:22
Symbols: manger, chalice and host

DECEMBER 24
Jesus is the *Light of the World*: John 1:1-14
Symbols: candle, flame

SYMBOLS — O ANTIPHON HOUSE

O Wisdom

O Lord and Ruler

O Root of Jesse

O Key of David

O Rising Dawn

O King of the Nations

O Emmanuel

Christmas Eve

Christmas Day

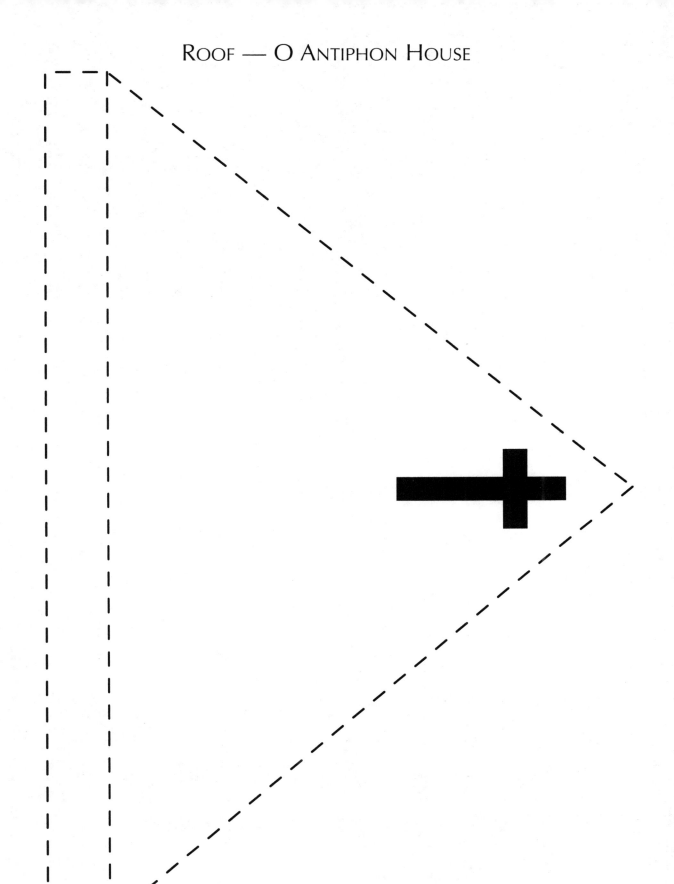

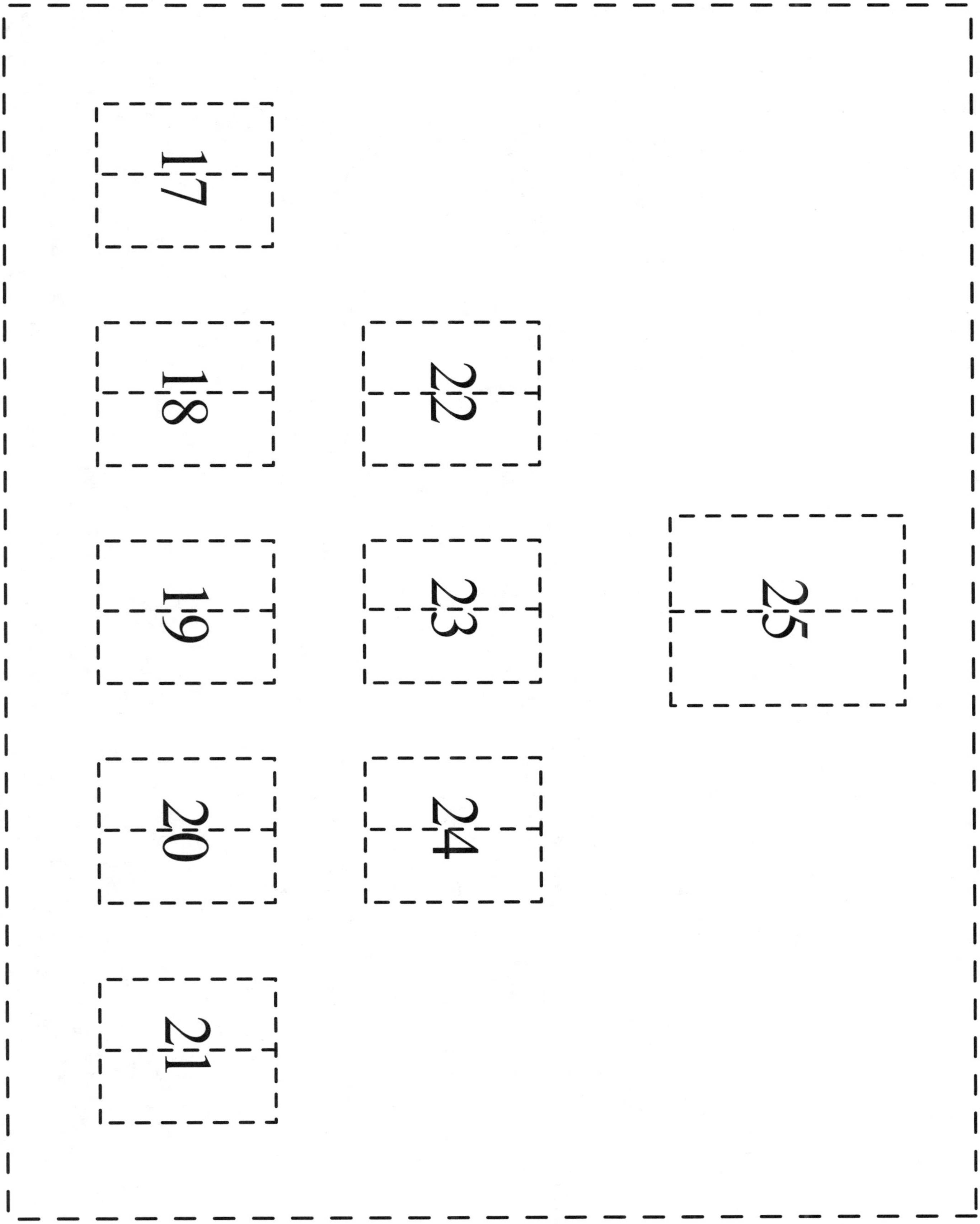

17

18

22

19

23

25

20

24

21

17

21

18

22

19

23

25

20

24

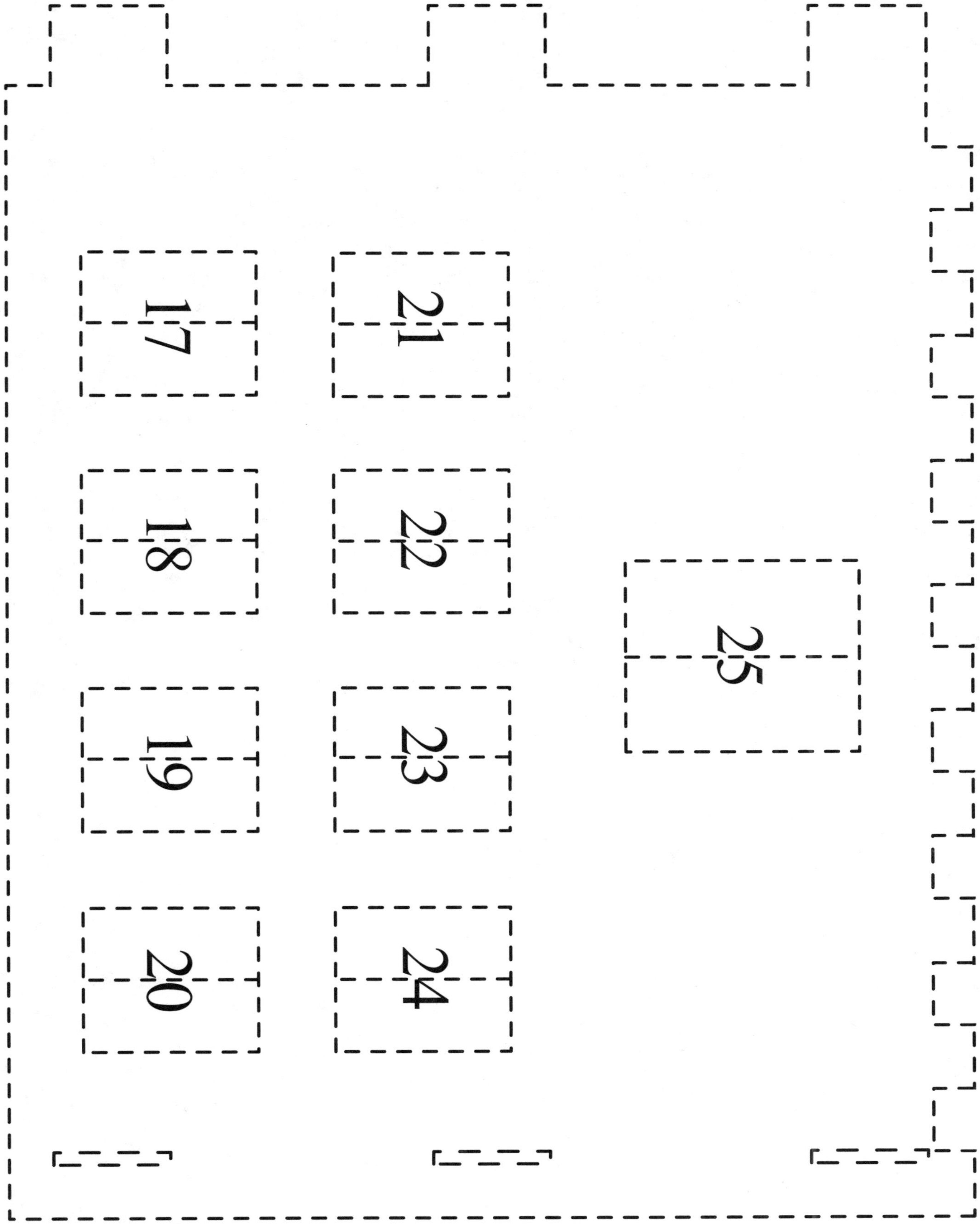

THE LITURGY OF THE HOURS

Christ taught us to pray always without becoming weary. This public prayer of the Church sets aside certain times of the day for prayer. In this way, the day is made holy, and all daily tasks are given back to God. When gathered as a faithful community, the Liturgy of the Hours celebrates the Paschal Mystery of Christ. It prepares us for the reception of the Eucharist and enables us to continue the work of the Eucharist.

The Liturgy of the Hours follows a basic structure and incorporates readings from the psalms, canticles, and other passages from the Old and New Testaments.

The hours are best prayed in community, but may be prayed by individuals when it is not possible to pray in common. Parishes are encouraged to celebrate in community at least Morning and Evening Prayer. If your parish does not offer this liturgical prayer, perhaps a good start would be to pray Evening Prayer once a week during the season of Advent. As a special observance during Advent, you might gather with friends or family on a weekly basis to pray the Liturgy of the Hours. The Liturgy of the Hours is the prayer of the entire Church, which unites us with all the faithful throughout the world, as well as with the communion of saints in heaven.

Books for praying the Liturgy of the Hours, such as *Shorter Christian Prayer*, may be found at your local Catholic bookstore.

"Great is the Lord and most worthy of praise."

Psalms 48:1

"FEED THE HUNGRY"

Choose one of the corporal works of mercy each Advent as a focus for your family or parish. The following are suggestions for the corporal work "Feed the hungry," to help you and your family incorporate this act of mercy in your Advent traditions.

✛ For one evening each week, have a family meal with no interruptions (no TV, phone, etc.).

✛ Make that weekly Advent meal more significant by discussing a subject that is meaningful. Use the daily news, community happenings, Scripture (readings for the following Sunday), or even Church doctrine as discussion topics.

✛ If your family is very young, invite an elderly or single guest to join you.

✛ If you are an empty nester, invite a couple of college students who are away from home to dinner.

✛ If you live alone or are single, meet a friend or co-worker for a simple but leisurely restaurant meal.

✛ To make your observance of Advent more diverse, invite a person, couple, or family of a different culture to dinner and share your Advent customs with one another.

✛ During one of your weekly family meals, discuss a "hunger" you have experienced, how you dealt with it, and in what ways, if any, it has changed you.

✛ Offer to transport a nursing-home resident to your house for dinner. Have your guest describe his or her Advent memories.

✛ Teach about liturgical colors and celebrate the season of Advent by using the colors of Advent — purple and rose — in your table settings (tablecloth, napkins, and plates).

✛ Scan the parish pictorial directory and select someone "out of the blue" to join your family for dinner, "just because I've seen you in church but have never spoken with you."

✛ When inviting people to dinner, let your guests contribute to the meal by having them bring their favorite desserts, drinks, or appetizers.

✛ Invite yourself or your family to dine with someone — but YOU bring the dinner! They need only supply the table settings, etc.

 ✛ Read and study the Sunday Scriptures of Advent as part of your family meal.

✛ Use this Grace Before Meals to distinguish Advent as a special season:

Bless, O God, this food and drink that you have given us for our bodily well-being. Give us also the grace of a holy Advent so that we can open our hearts to the true food and drink you give us for our spiritual well-being. We ask this through Jesus Christ our Lord. Amen.

✛ Simplify your meals to be able to give to those less fortunate.

✛ Satisfy your hunger for peace by discussing with your family at your evening meal how each person can be a peacemaker in your family, school, workplace, neighborhood, etc. Then carry out that action.

✛ A Polish custom is to set an extra place at the table. This is a visual reminder that Christ and His family would be welcome at this "inn" should they knock on the door tonight.

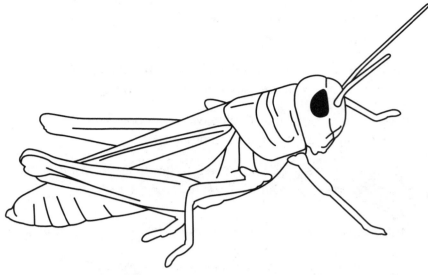

ST. JOHN THE BAPTIST

John the Baptist was Jesus' beloved cousin. He was a miraculous man from conception. Luke's Gospel says that John's mother, Elizabeth, was rather advanced in years when she came to expect John. Scripture also tells us that the infant leaped in his mother's womb when he heard Mary's voice.

John the Baptist was a man who chose to live simply. He spent much time in the desert, sometimes even reveling in the solitude. He lived off the land, most often noted for eating locusts (grasshoppers) and honey. John was sent to prepare the people for the coming of Christ, begging them to repent of their sins and follow in the footsteps of the One to come. He preached to all who would listen, and many received his baptism of repentance. John was a man who was devoted to God, and he was eventually beheaded for his faith.

DOING GOOD DEEDS

Whenever your children do a good deed during Advent, have them color in a footprint on the "Making My Way Through Advent With Good Deeds" page, as they "journey" toward the Christ Child at Christmas.

Another version of this activity would be to trace each family member's footprint, cutting out several footprints. Brown paper sacks are inexpensive and readily available for this activity. Each time a member of the family does a good deed, write it on the footprint. Tape the footprints to the wall, creating a path that leads toward your family Nativity scene.

Making My Way Through Advent With Good Deeds

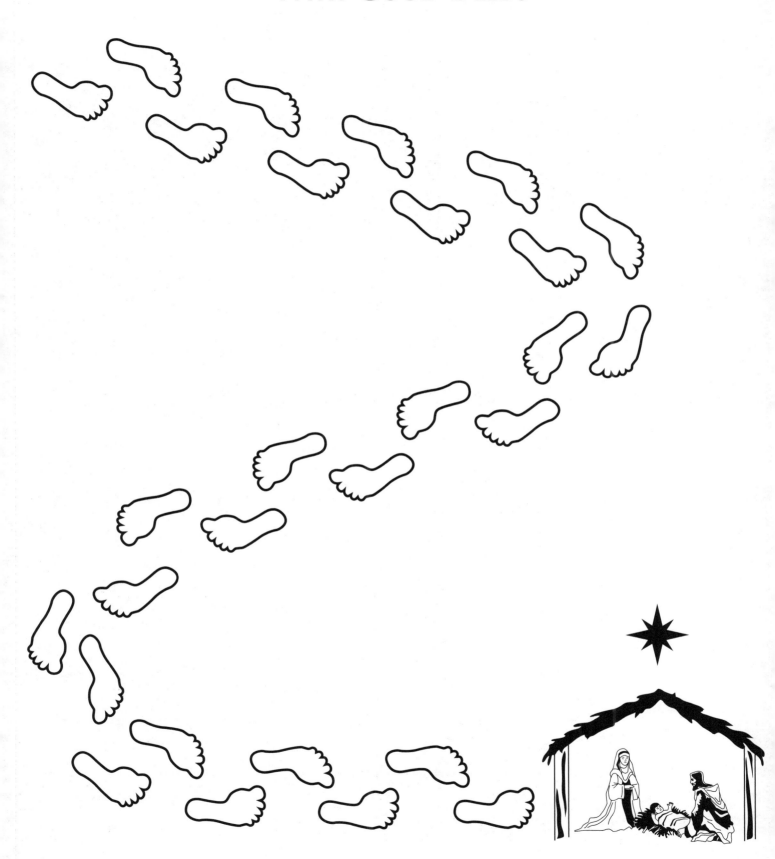

FOOT PATTERNS

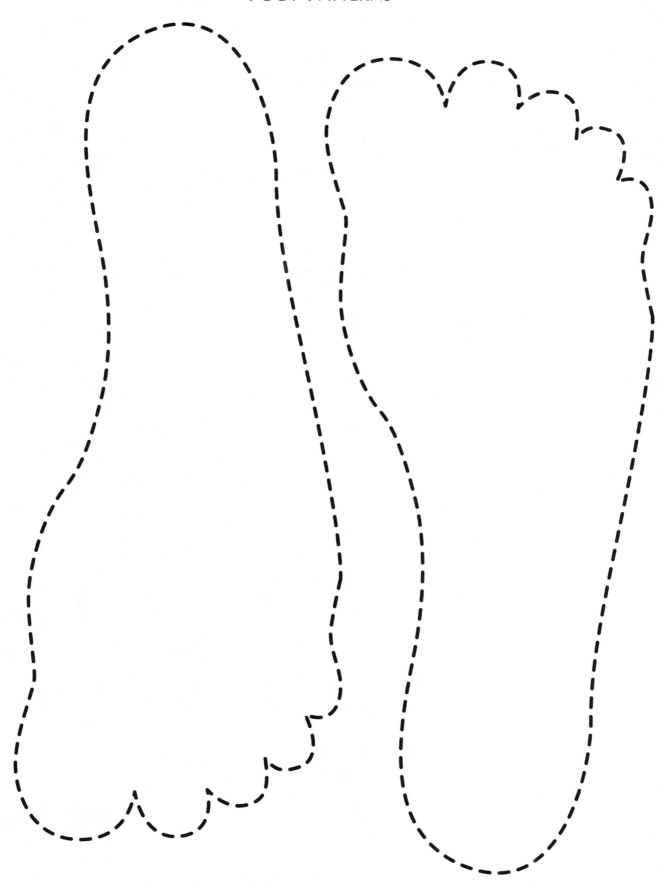

ST. JOHN THE BAPTIST

LAS POSADAS

Dating back to the 1580s, *Las Posadas* was created when a priest celebrated the story of the Nativity over a nine-day period, thereby helping to introduce Christianity to *Mexico*. It is now a celebration observed by both Catholics and Protestants. *Posada* means inn, lodging, or shelter. On the nights of December 16 through Christmas Eve, Mary and Joseph's search for a room in an inn is reenacted by processions of people.

Your family and friends can celebrate *Las Posadas*. Eight homes willing to host a party are chosen for eight nights. On the ninth night, the Christmas Eve procession ends at the church. Host families decorate their homes and invite their neighbors for the party. They have a piñata — filled with candy and nuts and perhaps small toys for children — to break at the end of the evening. Coffee, hot chocolate, and apple cider or punch, along with pastries, tamales, and sweet rolls or hot homemade doughnuts, are served.

Each night of *Las Posadas*, people meet near the designated home. Children dressed as Mary and Joseph, or carrying figures of them, lead a procession of pilgrims carrying lighted candles. When the pilgrims reach the house, the questions and answers begin between the hosts and guests.

A SAMPLE SERVICE FOR *LAS POSADAS*

The pilgrims knock on the door, and the hosts ask:
Who knocks so late at my door?

PILGRIMS: We are seeking shelter for the night. Please open your door for us.

HOSTS: No. You must leave. We do not know you.

PILGRIMS: I am Joseph, and this is my wife, Mary. She will soon give birth to God's Son. Please, we have been traveling a long way.

HOSTS: Then gladly we open our humble home to you. Welcome, Mary! Welcome, Joseph! Welcome, good pilgrims!

HOSTS *(praying)***:** O God, grant us the grace to turn away from the darkness of sin and to put on the light of Christ. May we humble ourselves as Christ humbled himself with his coming. Grant that with his final coming, he may find us worthy to live eternally with him. We ask this in his name. Amen.

Read Psalm 80, Luke 2:1-14, or traditional Advent Scriptures.

Sing an Advent hymn.

A JOURNEY WITH MARY AND JOSEPH
A CHILD'S PRAYER BY CATHERINE ODELL

In my heart, Mary and Joseph, I will journey with you and others for "Las Posadas."
Carrying lanterns, we sing joyfully and walk along with brave Joseph.
He leads poor, tired Mary on her little donkey.
> From house to house we go, asking to come in, to find a quiet place for the
> young mother who is about to give birth.
"We have no room. There's no room for you!"
On and on, we travel in hope, following an angel.
Finally, on the ninth night, we find shelter for the holy pilgrims.
Your holy child is born in a borrowed stable.
We will feast and sing and rejoice.
The long, hard journey has ended.
This newborn child shall bring us so much joy.

(From *Loyola Kids Book of Everyday Prayers*, by Catherine Odell and Margaret Savitskas [Loyola Press, 2002]. Reprinted with permission of Loyola Press. To order copies, call 1-800-621-1008 or go to www.loyolapress.com.)

Reading poetry or reflections, listening to music, and telling stories are other ways to celebrate the season of Advent with your family. Poetry, music, and storytelling are medias of the heart. These are wonderful ways to teach the faith indirectly.

STAR LIGHT

Out of necessity, Mary and Joseph made the journey from Nazareth to Bethlehem for the census, a journey they probably wouldn't have undertaken otherwise because of Mary's condition. Most likely they would have traveled in a caravan with families from Nazareth, along with others they would have met along the way. Traveling during the day and setting up a camp at night would have been their routine.

It would have been a long and arduous journey. After eating an evening meal and offering prayers, they would have settled for the night. Perhaps their gaze turned upward toward the night sky. What would have been their thoughts as they marveled at the magnitude of the night sky and the glories within? They must have wondered about their journey — perhaps silently worried about Mary's physical well-being, mixed with excitement in anticipation of their first child's birth. What was God asking of them and their child? What was in store for their family?

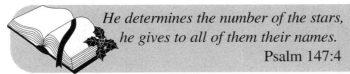

He determines the number of the stars,
he gives to all of them their names.
Psalm 147:4

We, too, journey through Advent on our lifelong pilgrimage. The night sky during the Advent season sparkles, as the days grow shorter and the nights grow more crisp and the skies clearer. The night sky holds many wonders of God's might and glory.

Spend time with the night sky, as an individual or as a family. Some of the brightest stars in our galaxy begin to rise in the east during Advent and dominate the winter sky. Learn the names of some of these stars and the constellations in which they lie. Learn to navigate your way around the night sky using these distinct stars and constellations. Investigate the stories and legends inspired by the stars and constellations. Members of your family may choose a star as their special star, as a reminder of God's goodness. Discover which planets are visible in the early morning or nighttime hours. Marvel at the magnitude of the glory within. A wonderful interactive sky chart is available online at www.skyandtelescope.com. This chart can help you determine what stars, planets, and constellations are visible in your area.

REFLECTIONS

1. As you turn your eyes toward the heavens, reflect on your own journey and that of your family. Where have you been? Where are you going? What is it that worries or concerns you? What is it that God has asked of you? Are you willing to place your fears in His hands? Are you grateful for His many blessings? Do we allow the stars to lead us to a sense of awe and wonder of God as Creator?

Advent is a time of darkness, like the night sky. It is illuminated by some of the brightest stars in our galaxy. What is amazing is that so much of the light we see twinkling in the night sky left those stars thousands of years ago!

2. Advent is a time of preparation to receive the Light of the World, Jesus Christ, into our hearts and lives. How well are we prepared to receive His light? How well do we let Christ's light shine in us and through us? Will our light continue to shine for others even if we are not present? Will our light illuminate the lives of others and bring them hope?

LUMINARIES

There is the *Mexican* tradition of luminaries (or "little fires") lighting the way during Advent, lining paths or sidewalks. Make luminaries by filling medium, brown paper bags (lunch bags) with an inch or so of sand or small stones. Place votive candles in holders in the sand or stones, and space them several feet apart. White gallon milk jugs with tops cut off also make good luminaries. They remind us that Christ is the Light of the World.

Include luminaries in your *Las Posadas* celebration.

CANDLES

Battery-operated votive candles work well instead of real candles, especially with children (at home or in the classroom) and the elderly. They are also useful when weather conditions are less than ideal for real candles or if supplemental oxygen is used by a member of your family. Battery-operated taper candles are also now available to use for your Advent wreath.

ADVENT WREATH

As an alternative, a three-dimensional wreath is available for families with small children or for the elderly. The felt Advent wreath has removable felt candles that are attached with Velcro. This wreath is available through most Catholic bookstores.

NATIVITY MATCH (GAME 1)

Rosary		Angel
		Christmas Star
Joseph		Manger
	Mary	
Stable	Nativity	
	Baby Jesus	

Nativity Match (Game 2)

White Lily		Dove
		Stone Tablets
Tongs and Hot Coal		Stone Watchtower
	Mother and Child	
Altar	Lamb	
	Ark	

SCENES FROM THE SEASON

SCRAPBOOK

Here is another way to commemorate the season. Take your religious-themed seasonal greeting cards, tear them in half, and keep the half with the religious scene. Hole-punch the corner of each one, and string them together using purple and/or rose-colored yarn or ribbon. You can add to this collection each year, and it becomes a beautiful tribute to this blessed season.

A variation would be to use the greeting-card scenes to tell the story of the Nativity by making a scrapbook that could become a family heirloom to be handed down through the generations.

Make the opening of the greeting cards a special event during Advent by opening them as a family after supper. Family members could take turns opening a card and reading it to the rest of the family. Then say a prayer together for the person who sent you the card. Waiting to open the cards until the family meal heightens the theme of anticipation of Advent.

THE CHRISMON™ TREE

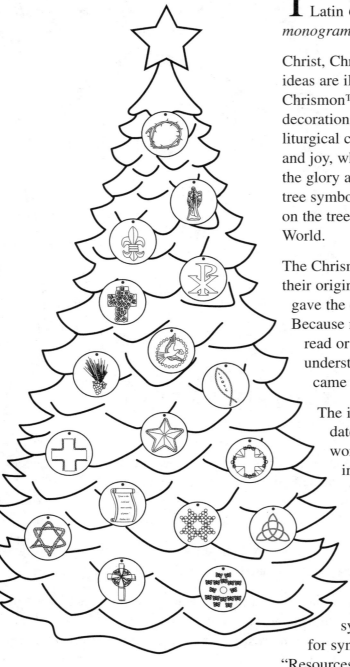

The word "Chrismon™" comes from the Latin *Christus* (meaning "Christ") and *monogramma* (meaning "monogram").

Christ, Christianity, or biblical and theological ideas are illustrated by the symbols used on the Chrismon™ Tree. Unlike the Jesse Tree, the decorations are in gold and white. White is the liturgical color of Christmas and signifies purity and joy, while gold, the color of kings, signifies the glory and majesty of God. The evergreen tree symbolizes everlasting life. The white lights on the tree illustrate Christ as the Light of the World.

The Chrismon™ Tree symbols, which trace their origins to the Church in the first century, gave the early Christians a sense of identity. Because most people of that time could not read or write, these symbols aided them in understanding the Gospel message that Jesus came to offer salvation to all people.

The idea of the Chrismon™ Tree itself dates back to 1957, when a Lutheran woman was asked to decorate the tree in her church. She used the early Christian symbols to reflect the traditions and beliefs of her faith. The copyright to the name "Chrismon™" is owned by her church, with the stipulation that Chrismons™ may never be sold for profit, although many patterns for the symbols may be purchased. Sources for symbol patterns may be found in "Resources" (pages 118-119).

The decorations may be made out of any type of materials; they may even be embroidered or cross-stitched.

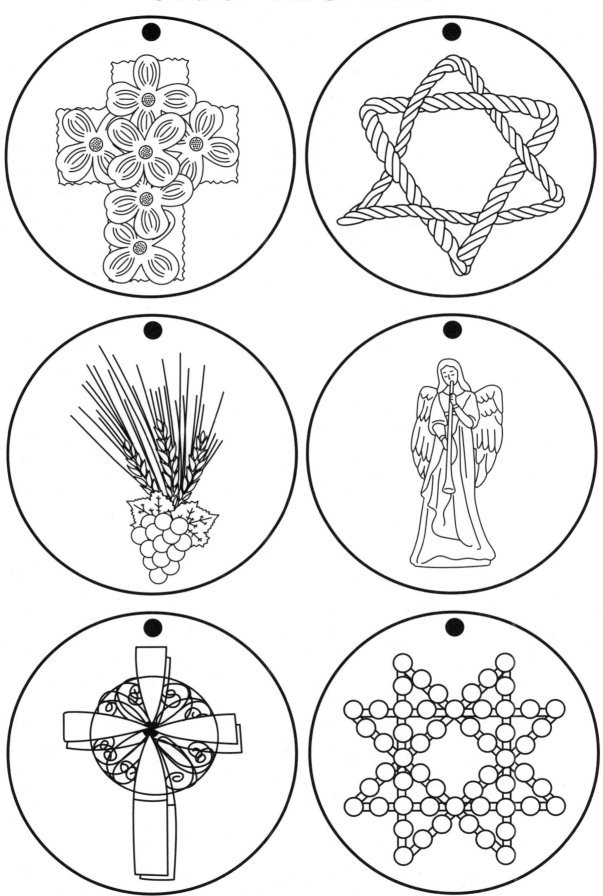

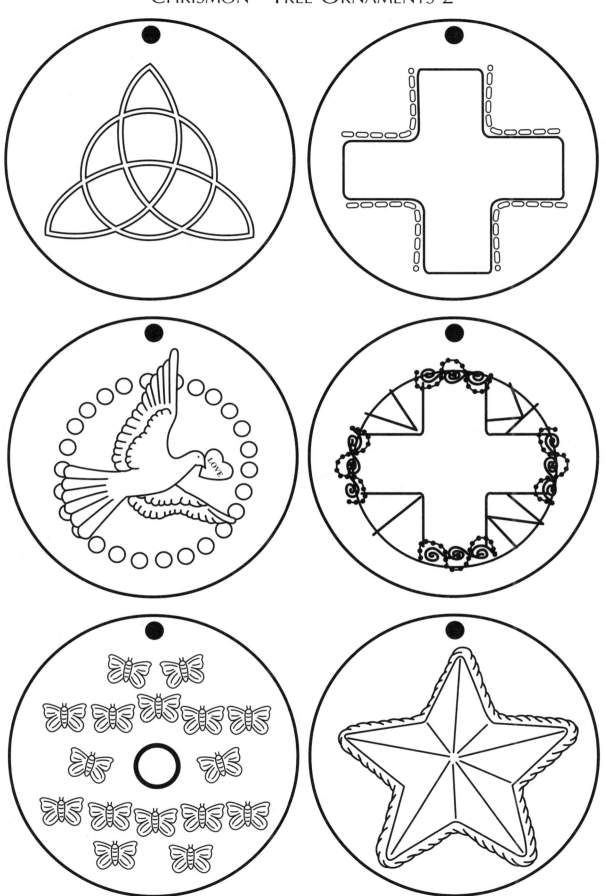

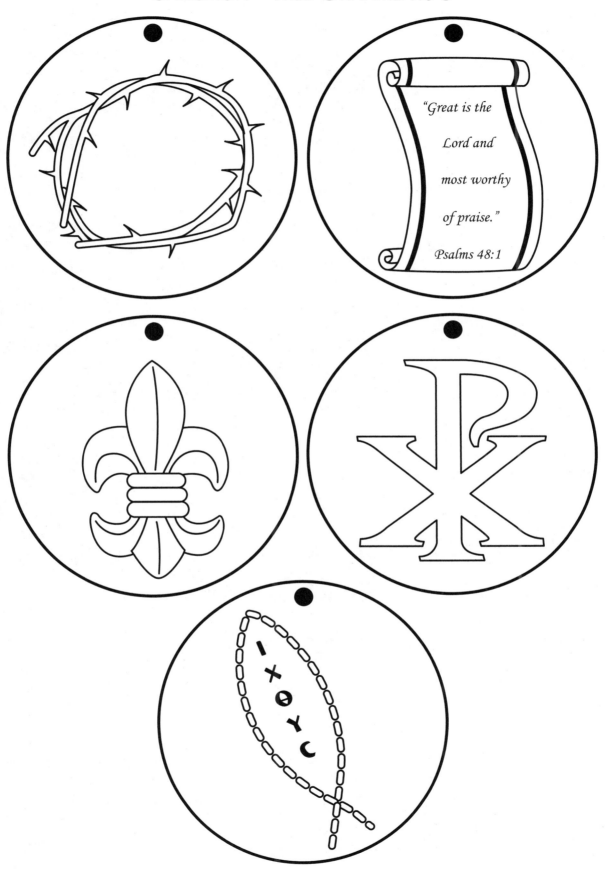

"Great is the Lord and most worthy of praise."

Psalms 48:1

CHRISMON™ TREE

OUR FAMILY CRÉCHE
(DRAW AND COLOR)

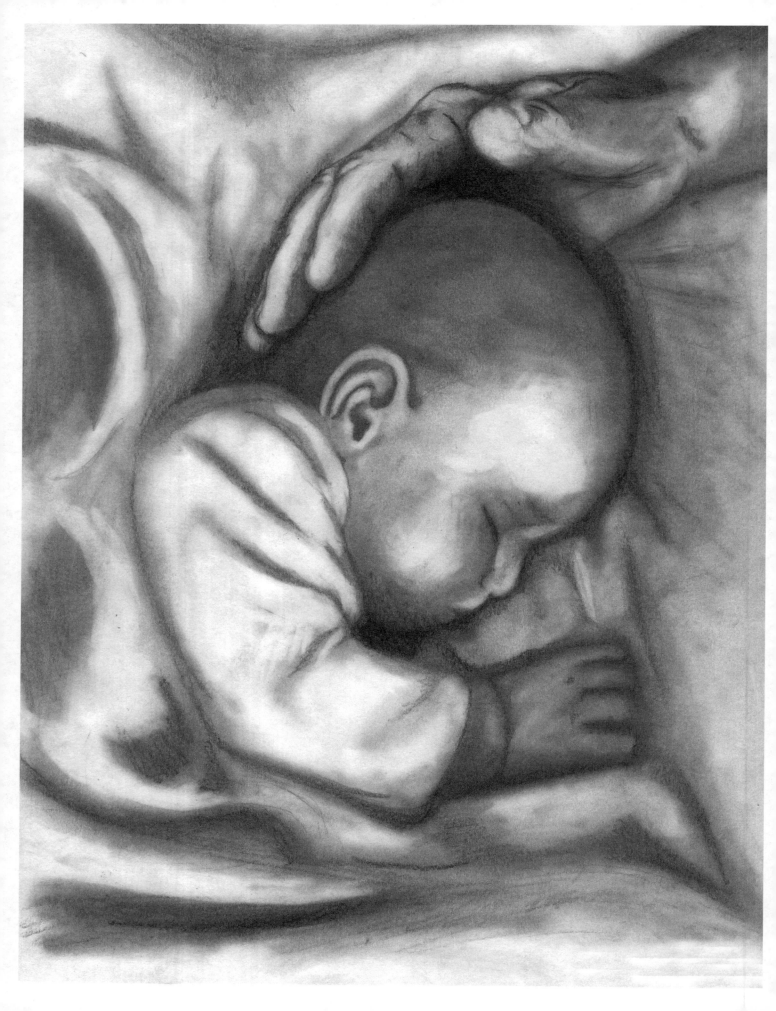

AND GOD REACHED DOWN
A POEM BY MARY T. BARNES

Stillness permeates the earth
As all creation waits with joyful anticipation.
Reaching from the heavens, Abba touches the child gently.
God's Son takes His first human breath.

As the Father's hand lovingly caresses the newborn,
A soft breeze is felt and the Spirit's whispered voice breaks the stillness.
"Be not afraid. I have something good and wonderful to tell each of you."

RESOURCES

BOOKS

Anderson, Raymond, and Georgene Anderson. *The Jesse Tree: Stories and Symbols of Advent.* Minneapolis: Augsburg Fortress Publishers, 1990.

Betty Crocker's Cookbook. Racine, WI: Western Publishing Company, Inc., 1969.

Bredkenridge, Marilyn. *Jesse Tree Devotions: A Family Activity for Advent.* Minneapolis: Augsburg Fortress Publishers, 1985.

Chiffolo, Anthony F. (compiler). *Advent and Christmas Wisdom from Padre Pio: Daily Scripture and Prayers Together With Saint Pio of Pietrelcina's Own Words.* Liguori, MO: Liguori Publications, 2005.

Christian Prayer. New York: Catholic Book Publishing Co., 1976.

Dobson, James C., Charles R. Swindoll, James Montgomery Boice, R. C. Sproul. *Christ in Christmas: A Family Advent Celebration.* Colorado Springs, CO: NavPress Publishing Group, 1989.

James, Darcy. *Let's Make a Jesse Tree.* Nashville, TN: Abingdon Press, 1988.

Kielly, Shiela and Sheila Geraghty. *Advent & Lent Activities for Children: Camels, Carols, Crosses, and Crowns.* New London, CT: Twenty-Third Publications, 1996.

Kruse, John V. (compiler). *Advent and Christmas Wisdom from Pope John Paul II: Daily Scriptures and Prayers Together with Pope John Paul II's Own Words.* Liguori, MO: Liguori Publications, 2006.

Merton, Thomas. *Advent and Christmas with Thomas Merton.* South Africa: Redemptorist Pastoral Publication, 2002

MUSIC

Candled Seasons: Music for Advent, Christmas, Epiphany, Candlemas (Audio CD). The University of Notre Dame Folk Choir and the Monastic Schola of Gethsemani Abbey. Notre Dame, IN: Ave Maria Press, 1994.

Gregorian Chant for Advent & Christmas in Latin and English (Audio CD). The Gregorian Chant Schola, St. Meinrad Archabbey. St. Meinrad, IN: St. Meinrad Liturgical Music, 1999.

A Season of Hope: Rediscovering Our Advent Heritage (Audio CD). Brotherhood of Hope. Somerville, MA: Brotherhood of Hope, 2004.

WEBSITES

"Advent — Waiting for Jesus Christ." Finding God: Our response to God's gifts. Loyola Press. **www.findinggod.org**.

"Chrismons™," by Dennis Bratcher. The Voice Institute: Biblical and Theological Resources for Growing Christians. **www.cresourcei.org/symbols/chrismon.html**.

"Chrismons™ Available Books." Ascension Lutheran Church. **www.chrismon.org/site/chrismon/booklist.php**.

"Readings and Psalms for the Month (New American Bible)." United States Conference of Catholic Bishops. **www.usccb.org/nab**.

Sky & Telescope online. **www.skyandtelescope.com**.

"Sunday Web Site." The Center for Liturgy at Saint Louis University. **www.liturgy.slu.edu**

"Symbol Patterns and Their Meaning," by Paul G. Donelson. **www.umcs.org/chrismons/patterns/index.htm**.